ELK HUNTING TIPS AND INFORMATION

Elk Hunting Tips and Information

A GUIDE TO SUCCESS IN THE FIELD

Philip Klassen

Serenity Publishers

Contents

Serenity Publishers ᵗᵐ

Requests for information should be addressed to:
Serenity Publishers, Box 1823 La Crete, Alberta T0H 2H0

Government of Canada ISBN Publication Data
Klassen, Philip, 1981-
Elk Hunting Tips and Information
Print ISBN: 978-1-0688515-0-6

Second Printing, 2024

To my daughters Bethannie and Brianna, who have shown an interest in elk hunting. Also, to my nephews Johnny and Logan who will join me on many elk hunts in the future, Lord willing.

1

Introduction to Elk Hunting

Elk hunting is a thrilling and rewarding experience that offers a unique challenge for hunters of all levels. Elk, also known as wapiti, are majestic creatures that roam the wilderness of Western North America, as far North as Alaska and South into Northern Mexico. They provide a true test of skill, patience, and endurance for those who pursue them. With their impressive antlers, powerful build, and elusive nature, elk have become a coveted trophy for many hunters.

A Brief History of Elk Hunting

Elk hunting has a rich history in North America, dating back to the early days of Native American tribes and European settlers. For centuries, elk were an essential source of food, clothing, and tools for many indigenous communities.

The arrival of European settlers brought new hunting techniques and firearms, which significantly impacted elk populations. By the early 20th century, elk numbers had declined drastically due to overhunting and habitat loss. However, conservation efforts and regulated hunting practices have helped restore elk populations, making them a thriving and sustainable game species today.

WHY HUNT ELK?

Elk hunting offers a unique combination of physical and mental challenges, making it an appealing pursuit for many hunters. Some reasons why hunters choose to pursue elk include:

- *Trophy quality:* Elk antlers are among the most impressive and sought-after trophies in North America. Elk are renowned for their impressive antlers, which make for a coveted trophy among hunters. The size, shape, and symmetry of an elk's antlers are key factors in determining its trophy quality. Here are some aspects that contribute to an elk's trophy quality:

- *Antler size:* Measured in inches, elk antlers can reach impressive sizes, with the largest bulls boasting antlers over 400 inches.

- *Point count:* The number of points on an elk's antlers is a key factor in trophy quality. Typical elk have 5-6 points per side, while trophy elk can have 7 or more.

- *Symmetry:* Well-matched antlers with similar shape and size are highly prized.

- *Circumference:* The circumference of the antler base, known as the "circumference at the smallest place between the first and second points," is another important factor.

- *Palmation:* The shape and size of the palm, or the flat part of the antler, can add to an elk's trophy quality.

- *Color and condition:* Antler color, ranging from light tan to dark brown, and the condition of the antlers, including any signs of wear or damage, can also impact trophy quality.

SCORING SYSTEMS

To evaluate and compare the trophy quality of elk, various scoring systems have been developed. The most widely used are:

• **Boone and Crockett Club (B&C) scoring system:**
This system measures the antler's length, circumference, and point count to calculate a total score.

• **Pope and Young Club (P&Y) scoring system:**
Similar to B&C, but with slightly different measurements and scoring criteria.

RECORD BOOK ELK

Timothy Carpenter's World record elk
September 21, 2023
https://www.boone-crockett.org

Elk that meet or exceed certain
scoring thresholds can
be considered "record book" elk,
earning a place in publications
like the Boone and Crockett
Club's
"Records of North American Big
Game" or the Pope and Young
Club's "Bowhunting Records."
Timothy Carpenter– Boone and Crockett

Remember, trophy quality is a personal preference, and many hunters value the experience and challenge of hunting elk and putting meat in the freezer just as much as the antlers themselves.

- *Meat:* Elk meat is highly prized for its flavor and nutritional value. Elk meat is rich in nutrients and is considered a healthy option. It has the lowest fat content among all commonly consumed meat. Our whole family enjoys elk meat, our favorites being steak and jerky I make at home.

- *Challenge:* Elk are elusive and require skill, strategy, and physical endurance to hunt successfully. Because of the challenge it presents and the persistence it takes, some Native Americans referred to elk as 'Ghosts of the forest.' They are notoriously difficult to hunt, and they can seem to just disappear while tracking them. Overall, elk hunting is a challenging and rewarding experience that requires a combination of physical and mental skills, as well as a deep respect for the animal and the environment.

- *Connection to nature:* Elk hunting allows hunters to connect with the wilderness and experience the beauty of nature. It often takes place in remote, pristine areas, allowing hunters to disconnect from urban life and reconnect with nature. Hunters develop a deep respect for the land, understanding the inter-connectedness of ecosystems and the importance of conservation. The physical demands of elk hunting require hunters to push their limits, developing a deeper connection to their own bodies and the natural world. For many hunters, it is a spiritual experience, con-necting them to nature, their heritage, and a sense of purpose. For myself, as soon as I get out into the forest and start pursuing elk, I am always struck by the awesomeness of creation, and how it is up to God to bring an elk within shooting range. He owns the cattle on a thousand hills, and He owns the elk as well.

Elk hunting also promotes a conservation ethos, encouraging hunters to support habitat con-servation, wildlife management, and sustainable hunting prac-tices, ensuring the long-term health of elk populations and their habitats. Through these as-pects, elk hunting offers a unique and profound connection to na-ture, fostering a deeper appreci-ation for the created world and our place within it.

Hunter admiring nature

- *Camaraderie:* Elk hunting often involves shared experiences and bonding with fellow hunters. The camaraderie of elk hunting is a unique and special aspect of the hunting experience. It's a bond that forms among hunters, built on shared experiences, challenges, and successes. Here are some ways that elk hunting fosters cama-raderie:

1. Shared adventure: Elk hunting is a challenging and exciting adventure that creates a sense of unity among hunters. Sharing the experience of tracking, stalking, and harvesting an elk creates a strong bond. I have done many solo hunts, but nothing beats evenings around the fire with friends and great food, regardless of if the day was successful or not.

2. Camp life: Hunting camps are a hub of activity, where hunters share stories, meals, and laughter. Camp life fosters a sense of community and belonging.

Many hands make lighter work

3. Teamwork: Elk hunting often requires teamwork, whether it's coordinating a stalk or helping to pack out an elk. Working together builds trust and reliance on one another.

4. Support and encouragement: Hunters often offer support and encouragement to their fellow hunters, helping to boost confidence and morale. There will be times you feel like giving up and it is always great to have a friend for support and encouragement. My worst experience as a hunter was being unable to recover a wounded animal. I felt so terrible that I thought I might never go hunting again. It was the encouragement from my wife that got me out there again and failure turned to success as I was fortunate to harvest my first elk a few weeks later.

5. Shared knowledge and expertise: Experienced hunters share their knowledge and expertise with newer hunters, passing on traditions and skills.

6. Celebrating successes: Hunters celebrate each other's successes, whether it's a first elk or a trophy bull.

7. Comradery in adversity: When faced with challenges like bad weather or difficult terrain, hunters come together to support each other and overcome obstacles.

8. Respect and trust: Hunting requires a high level of respect and trust among hunters, which strengthens the bond between them.

Never too old for 'elk fever'

9. Lifelong friendships: The camaraderie of elk hunting can lead to lifelong friendships, as hunters continue to hunt and share experiences together.

10. Hunting legacy: Hunting creates a sense of legacy, as hunters pass on their knowledge, skills, and traditions to the next generation. This is very important to me and something I enjoy doing. Taking out new hunters and giving them the experience of hunting is very gratifying. Daughters, friends, and nephews for now, but hopefully in a few years, grandsons as well.

The camaraderie of elk hunting is a unique and special aspect of the hunting experience, fostering a sense of community, belonging, and shared purpose among hunters.

TYPES OF ELK HUNTING

There are several types of elk hunting, each with its unique characteristics and challenges:

RIFLE HUNTING

The most common method, and the main focus of this book, using high-powered rifles to harvest elk at longer ranges. Rifle hunting elk is a popular and challenging way to hunt these magnificent animals. Here are some key aspects of rifle hunting elk:

Early morning river sit
Helen Klassen

1. Equipment: Rifles used for elk hunting are typically high powered, bolt-action, or semi-automatic rifles chambered in cartridges such as .30-06, .270, 7mm Rem Mag, .300 Win Mag, or .338 Win Mag. with a minimum of 3x magnification scope.

Elk-specific ammunition (e.g., 150-180 grain bullets) - Rifle sling and bipod or shooting sticks for stability.

Remember to check local regulations for specific gear restrictions and recommendations. It's also essential to practice marksmanship and familiarize yourself with your equipment before heading out on the hunt.

2. Long-range shooting: Elk hunting often requires long-range shooting, demanding accuracy, and precision.

3. Shot placement: Hunters must aim for vital organs, such as the heart, lungs, or brain, to ensure a quick and ethical harvest.

Remember, rifle hunting elk requires skill, patience, and respect for the animal and the environment. Always prioritize safety, follow local regulations, and practice ethical hunting practices.

ARCHERY HUNTING

A more challenging and intimate approach, using bows and arrows to get close to elk. Here are some key aspects of archery hunting elk:

1. Equipment: Archery hunters use bows and arrows specifically designed for hunting, with a focus on accuracy and penetration.

- Compound bow or recurve bow with a minimum draw weight of 50-60 pounds.
- Arrows (carbon or aluminum) with a minimum length of 27-30 inches.

- Broadheads (fixed or mechanical) with a minimum cutting diameter of 1 inch.
- Bow sight (fixed or adjustable) with a level and stabilizer.
- Arrow rest (drop-away or fixed) - Bow release or finger tab.
- Arm guard and finger tab for protection and consistency.

Elk vitals location

2. Scouting and preparation: Pre-season scouting, and preparation are crucial to locate elk habitats, identify patterns, and understand behavior.

3. Stalking and approaching: Archery hunters must use stealth, camouflage, and wind direction to stalk and approach elk undetected, getting within close range (typically 20-40 yards).

4. Shot placement: Archers must aim for vital organs, such as the heart, lungs, or liver, to ensure a quick and ethical harvest.

5. Close-range encounter: Archery hunting provides a unique, close-range encounter with elk, allowing hunters to experience the animal's size, strength, and majesty up close.

Remember, archery hunting elk requires a deep respect for the animal, the environment, and the hunting tradition. Always prioritize safety, follow local regulations, and practice ethical hunting practices.

MUZZLELOADER HUNTING

A traditional and historic method, using black powder rifles to add an extra layer of difficulty. Muzzleloader elk hunting is a unique and challenging way to hunt elk. Here are some key aspects of muzzleloader elk hunting:

1. Traditional equipment: Muzzleloader hunters use traditional black powder rifles, replicating the experience of early hunters.

2. Single shot: Muzzleloaders fire a single shot, making each shot count and emphasizing the importance of accuracy and patience.

3. Close-range encounter: Muzzleloader hunting typically involves close-range encounters (50-100 yards), providing an intimate experience with the elk.

4. Shot placement: Hunters must aim for vital organs, such as the heart, lungs, or liver, to ensure a quick and ethical harvest.

5. Historical connection: Muzzleloader hunting provides a historical connection to early hunters and the traditional ways of hunting elk.

There are **three basic categories of muzzleloading guns**: flintlock, caplock, and inline. The types of muzzleloaders available include flintlocks, percussion cap rifles, muskets, and inline muzzleloaders. Traditional muzzleloaders are either long-barreled and full-length stocked Pennsylvania or Kentucky rifles, or short-barreled and half-stocked Hawken or Plains rifles. Modern muzzleloading firearms range from reproductions of sidelock, flintlock and percussion long guns, to in-line rifles that use modern inventions such as a closed breech, sealed primer and fast rifling to allow for considerable accuracy at long ranges.

Remember, muzzleloader elk hunting requires a deep respect for the animal, the environment, and the hunting tradition. Always prioritize safety, follow local regulations, and practice ethical hunting practices.

BACKCOUNTRY HUNTING

Wilderness beauty
Helen Klassen

Venturing into remote wilderness areas, often requiring hiking, and camping to reach elk habitats. Backcountry hunting is a challenging and rewarding experience that takes hunters into the remote wilderness areas where elk roam free. Here are some key aspects of backcountry elk hunting:

1. Remote locations: Backcountry hunting takes place in remote, hard-to-reach areas, often requiring long hikes or horseback rides to access.

2. Physical demands: Hunting in the backcountry requires a high level of physical fitness, as hunters must navigate rugged terrain, climb steep inclines, and pack out heavy loads.

3. Self-sufficiency: Backcountry hunters must be self-sufficient, carrying all their gear, food, and water into the wilderness.

4. Camping and wilderness skills: Hunters must have experience with camping, wilderness survival, and outdoor skills, such as navigation and first aid.

5. Spot-and-stalk hunting: Backcountry hunting often involves spot-and-stalk hunting, where hunters locate elk and then stalk them to get within shooting range.

6. Long-range shooting: Backcountry hunting may also require long-range shooting, demanding accuracy, and precision.

7. Mental preparation: Backcountry hunters must be mentally prepared for the challenge, staying focused and patient during long days and challenging conditions.

8. Solitude and wilderness experience: Backcountry elk hunting provides a unique opportunity to experience the solitude and beauty of the wilderness.

9. Personal challenge: Backcountry hunting is a personal challenge, requiring hunters to develop skills, overcome obstacles, and push themselves to succeed.

Whether you're a seasoned hunter or just starting out, elk hunting offers a unique and rewarding experience that will test your skills, challenge your limits, and leave you with unforgettable memories. In the following chapters, we'll delve into the essential skills, strategies, and knowledge necessary to succeed on your elk hunting adventure.

2

Understanding Elk Behavior

To hunt elk effectively, it's crucial to understand their behavior and habitat. Elk are social animals that live in herds, led by a dominant cow. They are most active during early morning and late evening hours, and they tend to avoid areas with high human activity. Elk are also excellent swimmers and can often be found near water sources.

Elk behavior can be described as follows:

CALVING SEASON (MID-MAY TO EARLY JULY)

During calving season, elk exhibit the following behavioral patterns:

- They move around widely at night to feed in areas with the best grazing opportunities.

- During the day, they prioritize security and cover.

- At night, they prioritize food and water.

- They often form big herds of up to a hundred elk at night to feed.

- They separate into smaller harems as they head towards the trees or brush.

Elk calving season, is a critical period when female elk (cows) give birth to their young (calves). During this time:

1. Cows seek secluded areas with adequate food, water, and cover to calve. Secluded areas provide protection from predators like bears, wolves, and mountain lions, which pose a significant threat to newborn calves. Dense vegetation, like forests and shrubs, provides cover and concealment for cows and calves, making it harder for predators to detect them. Cows avoid areas with high human activity, such as trails and roads, to minimize stress and potential threats to their calves. Secluded areas also offer a sense of security and comfort for cows, allowing them to focus on caring for their newborn calves without distraction.

2. They become more solitary and protective of their calves. By separating from the larger herd, cows reduce the risk of their

calves being trampled, injured, or adopted by other females. This solitary behavior typically lasts for several weeks or even months, until the calf is strong enough to accompany its mother back to the larger herd.

3. Calves are born with their eyes open and are able to walk within the first hour of birth. Calves instinctively seek shelter and conceal-ment, often hiding in vegetation. As they gain strength, calves begin to explore their surroundings, investigating their environment, and they start to play, frolic, and run, developing their motor skills and strength.

4. Cows are very defensive of their calves and may charge if they feel threatened.

5. Calves are vulnerable to predators like bears, wolves, and moun-tain lions.

6. Cows will often leave their calves hidden in vegetation while they forage for food.

7. Calves begin to accompany their mothers on foraging trips at around 2-3 weeks old.

8. The calving season is a time of high energy demand for cows, as they nurse their calves and replenish their energy reserves.

Remember, it's essential to respect elk during this sensitive period and maintain a safe distance to avoid disturbing them. Enjoy observing from afar and appreciate the wonder of new life in the elk population!

PRE-RUT (AUGUST AND EARLY SEPTEMBER)

Contented elk herd –late summer

- Bulls are more likely to investigate bugles and cow calls.

- Bulls are more aggressive and vocal.

- Bulls are not yet herded up.

- Younger bulls are often seen with cows.

- Solo bulls are getting restless as the rut draws near.

These increased bull activities signal the start of the pre-rut period. During this time, bulls are establishing dominance, preparing for the rut, and vying for mating opportunities.

Pre-rut elk behavior, is characterized by:

1. *Increased bull activity:* Bulls become more active, vocal, and aggressive as they prepare for the upcoming rut.

2. *Solo bull behavior:* Mature bulls often wander alone, searching for cows and testing their dominance.

3. *Young bull behavior:* Younger bulls may still be with their mothers or in small bachelor groups, but they're starting to venture out and explore.

4. *Cow behavior:* Cows are still in small family groups, but they're becoming more receptive to bull advances.

5. *Bugling:* Bulls start bugling, a high-pitched call to announce their presence and attract cows. Bulls begin to bugle more often, testing their voices and announcing their presence to other elk.

6. Rubbing and marking: Bulls begin rubbing their antlers on trees and marking their territory with urine and feces.

7. Sparring: Bulls engage in sparring matches to establish dominance and test strength.

8. Traveling: Elk may travel longer distances in search of food, water, potential mates, and exploring their surroundings.

9. Vocalization: Elk are more vocal, with bulls making high-pitched calls and cows responding with softer chirps. Bulls make various calls, including grunts, chirps, and high-pitched screams.

10. Increased movement: Elk are more active during this period, making them more visible and audible to hunters and observers as they venture out of dense cover and into open areas.

11. Changes in habitat use: Bulls may start using different habitats or areas, such as ridges, meadows, or valleys.

12. Increased interaction with cows: Bulls begin to show interest in cows, approaching and courting them.

13. Aggressive behavior: Bulls become more aggressive, chasing other bulls and cows, and defending their territory.

Remember, understanding pre-rut behavior helps hunters and wildlife enthusiasts anticipate and prepare for the upcoming rut, when elk are most active and vocal.

IN RUT (MID-SEPTEMBER)

Two bulls getting ready to spar

- Most cows come into heat.

- Bulls are very vocal and aggressive.

- Herd bulls will flee with their cows from what they perceive as competition.

- Satellite bulls will hover around herd bulls with harems.

Elk in rut behavior, is characterized by:

1. Intense bugling: Bulls bugle frequently, often in a high-pitched, screaming tone, to announce their presence and attract cows.

2. Aggressive behavior: Bulls become highly aggressive, fighting each other for dominance and mating rights.

3. Herding: Dominant bulls gather and fiercely protect their harems of cows, chasing away other bulls.

4. Chasing: Bulls relentlessly chase cows in heat, often running them for miles.

5. Mating: Bulls mate with multiple cows in their harem, often in a matter of minutes.

6. Dominance displays: Bulls engage in loud bugling, pawing, and urine-soaked displays to assert dominance.

A bull chasing his cows

7. Reduced feeding: Bulls focus on mating and defending, neglecting food and water.

8. Increased movement: Elk move more frequently, making them more visible and audible.

9. Vocalization: Elk are at their most vocal, with bulls bugling, cows chirping, and calves bleating.

10. Hierarchical structure: A clear dominance hierarchy emerges, with dominant bulls leading the way.

11. Cows in heat: Cows become receptive to mating, and bulls fiercely compete to mate with them.

12. Tending behavior: Bulls tend to their harems, keeping cows close and chasing away potential rivals.

13. Chasing satellite bulls: Dominant bulls chase away smaller, satellite bulls that try to steal mating opportunities.

Remember, understanding elk in rut behavior helps hunters and wildlife enthusiasts appreciate the intensity and complexity of elk social dynamics during this critical mating period.

POST-RUT (OCTOBER AND LATER)

- Most breeding has taken place and the cows are gathering into bigger herds.

- Bulls will converge on these cows from miles away.

- Elk are more agitated and hence more vocal.

- Finding them can be easy if you're within earshot; otherwise, it can take a lot of hiking to locate them.

Post-rut elk behavior, is characterized by:

1. *Decreased bugling:* Bulls bugle less frequently, as the rut winds down.

2. *Dispersal:* Bulls disperse from their harems, and cows begin to form larger herds.

3. *Reduced aggression:* Bulls become less aggressive, as the mating season ends.

4. *Feeding focus:* Elk prioritize feeding, replenishing energy reserves depleted during the rut.

5. *Herd formation:* Cows, calves, and younger bulls form larger herds, often led by experienced cows.

6. *Bull bachelor groups:* Mature bulls form small bachelor groups, resting and recovering from the rut.

7. *Decreased movement:* Elk movement slows, as they focus on feeding and resting.

8. Vocalization decrease: Elk vocalizations decrease, with only occasional bugling or chirping.

After a long rut, bulls join up to survive the winter

9. Habitat shift: Elk may move to lower elevations or different habitats, seeking food and shelter.

10. Winter preparation: Elk prepare for winter, growing thicker coats and storing fat reserves.

11. Cows and calves reunite: Cows and calves that were separated during the rut reunite, re-establishing family bonds.

12. Bulls regain energy: Bulls recover from the physical demands of the rut, regaining strength and energy.

13. Elk become more secretive: Elk become more elusive, avoiding human detection and disturbance.

14. Less visible: Elk become less visible, as they move to more secluded areas and reduce their activity.

Remember, understanding post-rut elk behavior helps hunters and wildlife enthusiasts recognize the transition from the intense mating season to the more relaxed winter months, when elk prioritize survival and preparation for the next year's rut.

WINTER (NOVEMBER TO APRIL)

Elk have adapted to survive harsh winter conditions by developing the following habits:

- *Cold temperatures:* Elk grow a thicker coat of fur to provide insulation during winter.

- *Deep snow:* They migrate to lower elevations where there is less snow and more food available.

- *Energy conservation:* They reduce activity during extreme cold to conserve energy.

- *Limited water and food:* They conserve water by reducing intake and eating snow. They feed on woody browse, such as twigs and bark, when grasses and other vegetation are buried under snow.

- *Predator avoidance:* They tend to form larger groups, which helps them conserve heat and reduce predation risk.

- *Food scarcity:* They build up fat reserves during the fall to draw upon for energy during the winter.

During winter, elk rely on their survival instincts to endure harsh conditions. These instincts help elk survive the harsh winter months, allowing them to thrive until spring arrives.

3

Pre-Season Preparation

Before the hunting season begins, it's essential to prepare yourself and your gear. This includes:

PHYSICAL CONDITIONING

Elk hunting requires stamina and endurance, so start training early.

Elk hunting requires a high level of physical conditioning due to the demanding terrain, long distances, and heavy loads. Hunters need to be prepared for:

1. Cardiovascular endurance: Hiking uphill, carrying heavy packs, and navigating rugged terrain demands a strong heart and lungs.

2. Muscular strength and endurance: Carrying heavy rifles, packs, and elk meat requires significant upper body strength and endurance.

3. Leg strength and endurance: Hiking long distances, climbing steep terrain, and navigating uneven ground demands strong legs.

4. Core strength: A strong core is essential for stability, balance, and carrying heavy loads.

5. Flexibility and mobility: Hunters need to be able to move freely and comfortably in various terrain and weather conditions.

Taking advantage of stairs at work
Helen Klassen

6. Balance and coordination: Navigating uneven terrain, crossing streams, and climbing requires good balance and coordination.

7. Mental toughness: Elk hunting can be mentally demanding due to the physical challenges, weather conditions, and pressure to succeed.

To prepare, hunters should engage in regular:

- Cardiovascular exercise (running, hiking, cycling)

- Strength training (weightlifting, bodyweight exercises)

- Endurance training (long hikes, backpacking)

- Flexibility and mobility exercises (stretching)

- Balance and coordination exercises (balance training, obstacle courses)

- Mental preparation (visualization, mindfulness, goal setting)

It's essential to start training well in advance of the hunting season to build up your physical conditioning and mental toughness. This will help ensure a safe and successful elk hunting experience. Being in good physical condition could be the difference of being successful or not. Being able and willing to go to areas that others don't, could mean finding elk that have moved out of heavily hunted areas and into thicker and denser brush. I have found in the past that not having the stamina and endurance it requires, has kept me from going places where I knew there were elk and thus missing out on opportunities to harvest a bull.

Preparing physically for elk hunting season can be achieved through a combination of cardiovascular exercise, strength training, and flexibility workouts. Here are some simple and easy-to-do exercises at home to get you started:

Cardiovascular Exercises:

1. Brisk Walking: Walk uphill or on stairs for 30 minutes, 3 times a week.

2. Jumping Jacks: 3 sets of 30 seconds, 3 times a week.

3. Burpees: 3 sets of 10 reps, 3 times a week.

4. Mountain Climbers: 3 sets of 30 seconds, 3 times a week.

Strength Training Exercises:

1. Squats: 3 sets of 10 reps, 3 times a week.

2. Lunges: 3 sets of 10 reps (per leg), 3 times a week.

3. Push-ups: 3 sets of 10 reps, 3 times a week.

4. Planks: 3 sets of 30-second hold, 3 times a week.

5. Dumbbell Rows (using water bottles or cans): 3 sets of 10 reps, 3 times a week.

Flexibility and Mobility Exercises:

1. Leg Swings: Front and back, 3 sets of 10 reps.

2. Hip Circles: 3 sets of 10 reps.

3. Calf Raises: 3 sets of 15 reps.

4. Arm Circles: 3 sets of 10 reps.

Elk Hunting Specific Exercises:

1. Backpack Walks: Wear a loaded backpack (20-30 lbs) and walk uphill or on stairs for 30 minutes.

2. Uphill Sprints: Sprint uphill for 30 seconds, rest for 1 minute, and repeat for 30 minutes.

Remember to: - Start slowly and increase intensity and duration as you progress.

- Listen to your body and rest when needed.

- Stay hydrated and fuel your body with a balanced diet.

RIFLE PREPERATION

- *Rifle accuracy:* Practice shooting at long ranges to ensure accuracy. Rifle accuracy is crucial for hunting, as it ensures a quick and ethical harvest. Accuracy depends on various factors, including:

- Rifle and ammunition quality.

- Shooter skill and technique.

- Shooting position and stability.

Different shooting positions require adaptability and practice:

1. Offhand (standing): Requires strength, balance, and control.

2. Kneeling: Provides stability but demands flexibility and comfort.

3. Prone (lying down): Offers maximum stability but can be uncomfortable.

4. Sitting: Allows for relaxation but requires a stable rest.

5. From a tree stand or elevated position: Demands attention to safety and accuracy.

Hunter at sitting position

To improve rifle accuracy for hunting:

- Practice regularly, focusing on proper technique and fundamentals.

- Use quality rifles and ammunition suitable for hunting. When I'm dialing in my rifle before the hunt, I always use the same ammunition I will use on the hunt. This guarantees more consistency and eliminates any surprises.

- Master various shooting positions and adapt to different terrain and situations. We all want to have a rest or anchor point for our rifle when the critical time comes, but the truth is, elk can come in so quickly that there is not always time to set up. If different shooting positions have been practiced before hand, there is less chance of missing that kill shot.

- Develop muscle memory through repetition and practice.

- Learn to read wind, distance, and target movement to make accurate shots.

- Consider using a rifle scope or sights to enhance accuracy.

- Always prioritize safety and ethical hunting practices.

Remember, accurate shooting is a skill that takes time and effort to develop. Practice and dedication are essential for a successful and ethical hunting experience.

GEAR SELECTION

Choose appropriate clothing, boots, and gear for the terrain and weather conditions. Gear selection for elk
hunting is crucial for a successful and comfortable experience.

Here are some essential items to consider:

1. Rifle:
Rifle Selection for Elk Hunting:

- *Caliber:* .270, .30-06, .300 Win Mag, .338 Win Mag, and 7mm Rem Mag are popular choices.

- *Action:* Bolt-action rifles are preferred for their accuracy and reliability.

Bolt action hunting rifle

- *Barrel Length:* 24-26 inches for balance and maneuverability.

- *Stock:* Durable, weather-resistant materials like synthetic or wood.

- *Scope:* Quality optic with good magnification and light transmission

2. Ammunition:

- High-quality, heavy-bullet cartridges for effective harvesting.

Ammunition for Elk Hunting:

- *Bullet Weight:* 150-180 grains for .270 and .30-06, 180-220 grains for larger calibers.

- *Bullet Type:* Soft-point or controlled expansion bullets for effective expansion and penetration.

- *Cartridge Selection:* Choose a cartridge with a flat trajectory and sufficient kinetic energy (KE) for ethical harvesting.

- *Ballistics:* Consider the rifle's ballistic capabilities and the cartridge's performance at various distances. I always carry a ballistics chart in my pocket of the caliber, weight, and type of cartridge I use for quick reference out in the field. This has come in handy more than once, when having to shoot longer distances.

Popular Rifle and Ammunition Combinations for Elk Hunting:

- .270 Winchester with 150-grain bullets

- .30-06 Springfield with 180-grain bullets

- .300 Winchester Magnum with 200-grain bullets

- .338 Winchester Magnum with 225-grain bullets

- 7mm Remington Magnum with 160-grain bullets

Remember to:

- Check local regulations for specific caliber and ammunition requirements.

- Consider your rifle's capabilities and your shooting skills.

- Choose ammunition suitable for the expected shooting distances and elk size.

- Practice with your chosen rifle and ammunition to ensure accuracy and confidence.

3. Backpack:

When looking for a hunting backpack, consider the following key features:

- *Durability:* Look for high-quality materials, sturdy stitching, and reinforced stress points.

- *Comfort:* Choose a pack with padded shoulder straps, a hip belt, and a breathable back panel for comfort and support.

- *Water Resistance:* A waterproof or water-resistant design will keep your gear dry in harsh weather conditions.

- *Organization:* Multiple compartments, pockets, and attachment points help keep gear organized and accessible.

- *Capacity:* Select a pack with sufficient space for your gear, considering the length of your hunt and the equipment you need.

- *Weight Distribution:* A pack with a hip belt and compression straps helps distribute weight evenly, reducing fatigue.

- *Camouflage or Earth Tones:* A pack that blends with your surroundings helps maintain stealth.

- *Rifle or Bow Holder:* Consider a pack with a built-in rifle or bow holder for convenient transport.

- *Hydration Compatibility:* A pack with a hydration bladder sleeve and drinking tube ports keeps you hydrated on the go.

- *Adjustability:* Look for a pack with adjustable torso and shoulder straps to fit your body comfortably.

- *Noise Reduction:* Some packs feature noise-reducing materials or designs to minimize sounds while moving.
- *Gear Attachment Points:* Multiple attachment points for accessories like flashlights, knives, or first aid kits keep gear within reach.

Remember, the best backpack for you will depend on your specific needs, preferences, and hunting style.

4. Clothing:

Proper clothes for elk hunting are crucial for comfort, concealment, and success. Consider the following:

- *Camouflage:*

- Choose a pattern that matches your hunting environment (e.g., forest, mountain, or grassland).

- Consider a 3D leafy or branch-style camouflage for added concealment.

- *Earth Tones:*

- Stick to natural colors like green, brown, tan, and gray.

- Avoid bright colors, whites, and blacks.

- *Layering:*

- Wear moisture-wicking base layers for temperature regulation.

- Add insulating mid-layers (fleece or wool) for cold weather.

- Use a waterproof and breathable outer layer (jacket and pants).

- *Fabric:*

- Choose quiet, rustle-free fabrics like cotton, polyester, or nylon.

- Avoid noisy fabrics like nylon or polyester with a waterproof coating.

- *Pants and Jacket:*

- Look for durable, reinforced materials and construction.

- Consider pants with built-in knee pads for comfort.

- Insulating Layers:

- Add a warm hat, gloves, and scarf for cold weather.

- Use a face mask or balaclava for added warmth and concealment.

- *Accessories:*

- Use a camouflage or earth-toned hat and gloves.

- Add a camouflage face mask or neck gaiter for added concealment.

- Scent Control:

- Wear scent-controlled clothing and accessories.

- Use scent-eliminating products on your clothes and gear.

- Comfort and Mobility:

- Choose clothes that allow for ease of movement.

- Consider clothes with stretchy materials for comfort.

Remember to dress according to the weather and hunting conditions, and always prioritize comfort and concealment.

Some areas require you to wear some orange for safety reasons. Always follow your local regulations and requirements.

5. Footwear:
Proper footwear for Elk hunting is crucial for comfort, support, and success. Consider the following:

-Hunting Boots:

Choose sturdy, waterproof boots with good ankle support and traction. Look for boots with a breathable membrane (e.g., Gore-Tex or eVent). My favorite boots are the Irish Setter Elk Tracker.

-Insulation and Warmth:

Consider insulated boots for cold weather hunting. Look for boots with Thinsulate, Prima-Loft, or similar insulation.

-Tread and Traction:

Aggressive tread patterns provide better grip on various terrain. Look for boots with deep lugs and a self-cleaning design.

Irish Setter Elk Tracker boots
Helen Klassen

-Ankle Support:

High-top boots provide better ankle support and protection. Consider boots with a sturdy ankle collar and reinforced stitching.

-Comfort and Fit:

Choose boots with a comfortable, roomy toe box and a snug heel. Consider boots with a cushioned insole and breathable lining.

-Water Resistance:

Look for boots with a waterproof membrane and sealed seams. Consider boots with a water-resistant treatment for added protection.

-Durability:

Choose boots with high-quality materials and construction. Look for boots with reinforced stitching and rugged outsoles.

-Weight and Mobility:

Consider boots with a lightweight design for easier hiking. Look for boots with a flexible sole for improved mobility.

-Camouflage and Concealment:

Choose boots with a camouflage pattern or earth-toned color. Consider boots with a low-profile design to reduce visibility.

-Break-In Period:

Allow time to break in your boots before hunting. Wear them on shorter hikes to mold the boots to your feet. Don't make the mistake I did one year. I bought new boots a day before going out, and they were not broken in. I lasted two days. My feet were so sore, and I lost both my big toenails and had to shut the hunt down. Buy ahead of time, try them out and allow a break in period.

Remember, proper footwear can make a significant difference in your hunting experience. Invest in high-quality boots that meet your needs and provide comfort, support, and protection.

6. Sleeping Gear:

- Quality sleeping bag and pad for comfort. Up in Northern Alberta where I hunt, it can get quite cold in September. I always pack a small tent heater as well.

7. Cooking Gear:

This will depend on the length of your hunt and willingness to rough it. Some hot food can definitely make a hard day of hiking better.

Simple works for me
Helen Klassen

- Portable stove and fuel

- Cooking pot and utensils

8. Navigation:
- GPS device or smartphone with GPS app

- Map and compass

9. First Aid Kit:
- Basic medical supplies and emergency items

10. Hydration:
- Water bottle or hydration bladder

- Water purification tablets or filter

11. Optics:
- Binoculars for scouting and spotting

- Rangefinder for distance measurement

12. Game Bag:
- Durable, water-resistant bag for carrying harvested elk.

13. Multi-Tool or Pocketknife:
- Handy for various tasks and emergencies

14. Flashlight or Headlamp:

- For navigating in low light

15. Emergency Shelter and Fire Starters:

My camp is usually pretty basic.
Helen Klassen

- Lightweight tent and warmth sources (e.g., matches, lighter)

Remember to check local regulations for specific gear requirements and restrictions. It's also essential to consider personal preferences, terrain, and weather conditions when selecting gear.

SCOUTING

Research and scout potential hunting areas to identify elk habitats and migration patterns. Scouting for elk before hunting season is crucial to increase your chances of success. Here's a comprehensive guide to help you prepare:

1. Understand Elk Behavior:
- Study their habitat, migration patterns, and feeding habits.

- Learn about their social structure and communication.

2. Choose the Right Time:

- Scout during the pre-rut (July-August) and post-rut (October-November) periods.

- Avoid scouting during the peak rut (September) to minimize disturbance.

Elk scrape on a Poplar tree
Helen Klassen

3. Identify Elk Habitat:

- Look for areas with abundant food, water, and cover (timber, shrubs, and meadows).

- Pay attention to elevation, aspect, and terrain features.

4. Find Elk Sign:
- Look for tracks, scat, rubs, and wallows.

- Identify the age and sex of elk based on sign (e.g., large rubs indicate mature bulls).

5. Locate Elk Concentrations:
- Find areas with high concentrations of elk sign.

- Look for feeding areas, bedding grounds, and migration corridors.

6. Identify Travel Routes:
- Find game trails, ridges, and valleys used by elk.

- Pay attention to wind direction and thermals.

7. Set Up Trail Cameras:
- Place cameras in strategic locations (e.g., game trails, water sources, fences).

- Monitor camera footage to identify elk patterns and habits.

  Locations: Place cameras in areas with high elk activity, such as:
  - Game trails

  - Water sources

  - Food sources (meadows, acorn stands)

- Rubs and scrapes

Camera height: Mount cameras 3-4 feet off the ground to capture elk's chest or shoulder area for better identification.

Direction: Face cameras north to avoid sun glare and false triggers.

Sensitivity: Adjust sensitivity to minimize false triggers from wind, trees, or small animals.

Detection zone: Set the detection zone to 20-30 feet to capture elk as they approach.

Image quality: Use high-quality cameras with good image resolution (e.g., 12-20 megapixels) and fast trigger speeds (e.g., 0.5 seconds).

Memory and batteries: Use large memory cards and long-lasting batteries to minimize maintenance.

Lock and secure: Lock cameras to trees and use security boxes to prevent theft or tampering.

Check local regulations: Ensure compliance with local regulations regarding trail camera use.

Monitor and adjust: Regularly check cameras, adjust settings as needed, and move cameras to new locations to optimize results.

Remember to always follow ethical and responsible practices when using trail cameras for hunting.

8. Glassing and Observation:

- Use binoculars and spotting scopes to observe elk from a distance. Never use your rifle scope for spotting.

- Note their behavior, movement patterns, and habitat preferences.

9. Map and Record Findings:

- Create a detailed map of your scouting area.

- Record observations, elk sign, and habitat features.

10. Refine Your Strategy:

- Based on your findings, develop a hunting strategy.

- Choose the best locations, times, and tactics for your hunt.

Remember to respect private property and public land regulations during scouting. Always follow ethical and legal guidelines to ensure a successful and enjoyable hunting experience.

4

Hunting Strategies

Here are some effective elk hunting strategies:

CALLING

Elk calling techniques and strategies are used to mimic the sounds made by elk to attract them or to locate them during hunting season. Mouth reed or diaphragm calls are most popular, and my preferred ones. There have been some great advances on push button external call that work great for people that find mouth calls difficult. Slayer Calls has a great option for this.

Tips for using mouth reed calls:

- Start with a soft, gentle blow to avoid harsh sounds.

- Experiment with different tongue placements and movements to find what works best for you.

- Use a call with an adjustable reed tension to customize the sound.

- Practice regularly to develop muscle memory and improve your call. It is not fun for others to listen to me practicing, so I practice while driving by myself. It takes a lot of practice to learn the different calls, but it will pay off in the end. I have heard some pretty horrendous calls by other hunters when out in the bush, and elk are not fooled by this. The hardest one to learn for me has been the chuckle, and I will expand on that later.

Here are some techniques and strategies:

1. BUGLING:

- Mimic the high-pitched whistle of a bull elk.

- Use a bugle or a diaphragm call.

Warning all challengers

- Start with a soft, nasal sound and increase volume and pitch.

Here are some bugling techniques:

- The "Chuckle":
- Start with a soft, nasal "chu-chu-chu" sound.

- Gradually increase volume and pitch.

The elk "chuckle" is a vital call in an elk hunter's arsenal, used to mimic the sound of a happy, contented bull elk. It's a soft, low-pitched, throaty sound, often described as a gentle "brrr-mmm" or "grrr-uhh". Performing the elk "chuckle" using mouth reed calls requires a specific technique to produce the soft, throaty sound. Here's a step-by-step guide:

Some of my favorite reeds
Helen Klassen

1. *Choose the right mouth reed call:* Select a call with a soft, flexible reed designed for elk hunting.

2. *Hold the call:* Place the call in your mouth, with the reed facing towards the back of your throat.

3. *Position your lips and tongue:* Form an "O" shape with your lips and place the tip of your tongue behind the reed, close to the roof of your mouth.

4. *Blow air:* Gently blow air through the call, aiming for the reed's center. This produces a soft, gentle sound.

5. *Manipulate the reed with your tongue:* Subtly move your tongue to vibrate the reed, creating a throaty, chuckling sound.

6. Adjust air pressure: Vary the air pressure to control the pitch and volume, mimicking the natural inflections of an elk's chuckle.

7. Use your diaphragm to push out air: Do a short inhale between each chuckle, be careful not to inhale the
reed and choke on it. Do not use one breath to do a series of chuckles. This takes a lot of practice to perfect to get that authentic elk guttural sound by the short inhales between chuckles. Watching some YouTube videos on techniques can be very helpful.

Practice and refine: Repeat the process, fine-tuning your technique to achieve a soft, relaxed "brrr-mmm" or "grrr-uhh" sound.

By mastering the elk "chuckle" with mouth reed calls, you'll be able to effectively mimic the sounds of a contented bull elk, increasing your chances of attracting and engaging with bulls and cows alike. Remember to practice regularly to develop your skills and become a more effective elk hunter.

Tips:
- Practice the chuckle regularly to develop a natural, effortless sound.

- Experiment with different variations, such as adding a slight grunt or nasal tone.

- Use the chuckle in combination with other calls, like cow calls or calf calls, to create a realistic elk conversation.

- **Remember** to keep the chuckle soft and subtle, as elk have acute hearing and may be alarmed by loud or harsh sounds.

• The "Whistle":
- Make a high-pitched, ear-piercing whistle.

- Hold for 2-3 seconds, then release.

Ripping a bugle
Helen Klassen

• The "Bugle":
- Start with a low, guttural "buu" sound.

- Quickly transition to a high-pitched "gle" sound.

- End with a soft "uuu" sound.

• *The "Challenge":*
- Start with a loud, aggressive bugle.

- Follow with a series of rapid, high-pitched chuckles.

• **The "Location":**
- Use a soft, nasal bugle to locate elk.

- Repeat every 10-15 seconds to simulate a bull elk's territorial call.

- Use this call as your first call early in the morning. Just a simple long and loud bugle to see if you can get a bull to respond and give away his location.

• *The "Assembly":*
- Use a loud, aggressive bugle to assemble elk.

- Follow with a series of softer, more nasal bugles.

• *The "Rake and Bugle":*
- Use a raking call to simulate antlers on a tree.

- Follow with a loud, aggressive bugle.

• The "Sequence":
- Start with a soft, nasal bugle.

- Follow with a series of louder, more aggressive bugles.
    - End with a soft, nasal bugle.

Remember to vary your pitch, volume, and tone to simulate different bull elk and to keep the elk interested. Also, practice your bugling techniques before the hunting season to become proficient and effective.

2. COW CALLING:

- Mimic the chirping or bleating sound of a cow elk.

- Use a cow call or a diaphragm call.

- Make soft, high-pitched sounds, often in a series.

Here are some cow calling techniques:

• The "Chirp":
- Make a high-pitched, soft "chip" or "chirp" sound.

Primos® Hoochie
Mama Cow Call
Cabelas.ca

- Repeat every 10-15 seconds to simulate a cow elk's contact call.

• *The "Bleat":*
 - Make a soft, nasal "bleee" sound.

 - Repeat every 10-15 seconds to simulate a cow elk's bleat.

• *The "Mew":*
 - Make a soft, high-pitched "mew" sound.

 - Repeat every 10-15 seconds to simulate a cow elk's mew.

• *The "Whine":*
 - Make a soft, nasal "whine" sound.

 - Repeat every 10-15 seconds to simulate a cow elk's whine.

• *The "Sequence":*
 - Start with a soft, nasal chirp.

 - Follow with a series of softer, more nasal bleats.

 - End with a soft, nasal mew.

• *The "Conversational Call":*
 - Make a series of soft, nasal sounds, simulating a conversation between cow elk.

Remember to vary your pitch, volume, and tone to simulate different cow elk and to keep the elk interested. Also, practice your cow calling techniques before the hunting season to become proficient and effective. It's important to note that cow calling is generally used to bring in bulls, as they are attracted to the sound of a cow elk. However, cow calling can also be used to locate elk, as cows will often respond to the call.

3. CALF CALLING:

- Mimic the high-pitched squeaking sound of a calf elk.

- Use a calf call or a diaphragm call.

- Make soft, high-pitched sounds, often in a series.

Here are some calf calling techniques:

• *The "Squeak":*
- Make a high-pitched, soft "squeak" sound.

- Repeat every 10-15 seconds to simulate a calf elk's distress call.

• *The "Chirp-Squeak":*
- Start with a soft, nasal chirp.

- Follow with a high-pitched squeak.

• *The "Waa-Waa":*
- Make a soft, nasal "waa-waa" sound.

- Repeat every 10-15 seconds to simulate a calf elk's cry.

Lost calf calling for it's mother

• *The "Whine-Squeak":*
- Start with a soft, nasal whine.

- Follow with a high-pitched squeak.

• *The "Calf-in-Distress":*
- Make a series of high-pitched, soft squeaks and chirps.

- Simulate a calf elk in distress, trying to locate its mother.

• *The "Lost Calf":*
- Make a high-pitched, soft "calf-like" sound.

- Repeat every 10-15 seconds to simulate a lost calf elk.

- I have called in several bulls with the "Lost Calf" call.

• *The "Calf-Talk":*
- Make a series of soft, nasal sounds, simulating a conversation between a calf and its mother.

Remember to vary your pitch, volume, and tone to simulate different calf elk and to keep the elk interested. Also, practice your calf calling techniques before the hunting season to become proficient and effective.

Calf calling is often used to bring in cows, as they are highly protective of their calves and will often respond to the sound of a calf in distress. However, calf calling can also be used to bring in bulls, as they may see the calf as a potential threat or be attracted to the sound of a calf elk.

4. RAKING:

- Mimic the sound of antlers raking against trees.

Bull raking a pine tree
YouTube

- Use a raking call or a stick to scratch against a tree. Raking techniques for calling elk involve simulating the sound of antlers rubbing against trees, which is a common behavior among bull elk during the rutting season. Simply find a decent sized stick, then start thrashing a small sapling or bush with it. Elk can get pretty intense when they start tearing up a tree with their antlers, so put that same intensity into your raking. Stomp the ground, break branches, and make some noise. Here are some raking techniques:

- The "Rake and Bugle":

- Use a raking call to simulate antlers on a tree.

- Follow with a loud, aggressive bugle.

- The "Rake and Grunt":

- Use a raking call to simulate antlers on a tree.

- Follow with a low, guttural grunt.

- The "Rake and Chirp":

- Use a raking call to simulate antlers on a tree.

The thrill starts
Helen Klassen

- Follow with a soft, nasal chirp.

- The "Rake and Bleat":
  - Use a raking call to simulate antlers on a tree.

    - Follow with a soft, nasal bleat.

- The "Aggressive Rake":
  - Use a loud, aggressive raking call to simulate a dominant bull elk.

- The "Soft Rake":
  - Use a soft, subtle raking call to simulate a subordinate bull elk.

- The "Rake and Pause":
  - Use a raking call to simulate antlers on a tree.

  - Pause for 10-15 seconds to simulate a bull elk's momentary pause.

- The "Rake and Move":
  - Use a raking call to simulate antlers on a tree.

  - Move to a new location and repeat the raking call.

Remember to vary your raking techniques to simulate different bull elk and to keep the elk interested. Also, practice your raking techniques before the hunting season to become proficient and effective. One thing to be cognizant of while raking, be careful not to bump against anything metallic or plastic. This happened to me one time. I had a bull hung up at about 50 yards. I couldn't get him to step out and had a screaming match with him for a good 20 minutes. I was calling and raking, he was doing the same. With the adrenaline flowing and all the movement of raking, I hit my water bottle that was on the side of my pack a few times with the stick that I was using, and he never responded again.

Raking techniques can be used to:
- Locate elk

- Bring in bulls

- Bring in cows

- Simulate a dominant bull elk

- Simulate a subordinate bull elk

It's important to note that raking techniques should be used in combination with other calling techniques, such as bugling, cow calling, and calf calling, to create a more realistic and effective calling sequence.

5. GRUNTING:

During mating season, bull elk are known for their distinctive grunting sounds, often described as a loud, nasal "bugling" or "whistling". This vocalization is a key way for bulls to establish dominance, attract mates, and warn off rivals.

The grunting sound is usually accompanied by a visual display of strength, including raised antlers, pawing the ground, and a fierce stare. It's an impressive sight to behold!

- Mimic the low, guttural sound of a bull elk.

- Use a grunt call or a diaphragm call.

Grunting techniques for calling elk involve simulating the low, guttural sounds made by bull elk during the rutting season.

Here are some grunting techniques:
- *The "Low Grunt":*

  - Make a low, guttural "uuuu" sound.

  - Use a soft, nasal tone.

- *The "Aggressive Grunt":*
    - Make a loud, aggressive "GRRR" sound.

  - Use a deep, guttural tone.

- *The "Challenging Grunt":*
  - Make a series of low, guttural grunts.

  - Gradually increase volume and aggression.

- *The "Tending Grunt":*
  - Make a soft, nasal "uuuu" sound.

  - Use a gentle, soothing tone.

- *The "Rutting Grunt":*
  - Make a low, guttural "uuuu" sound.

  - Use a deep, aggressive tone.

- *The "Grunt and Bugle":*
  - Start with a low, guttural grunt.

  - Follow with a loud, aggressive bugle.

- *The "Grunt and Rake":*
  - Start with a low, guttural grunt.

  - Follow with a raking call.

- *The "Grunt Sequence":*
  - Make a series of low, guttural grunts.

  - Vary tone, volume, and pitch.

Remember to vary your grunting techniques to simulate different bull elk and to keep the elk interested. Also, practice your grunting techniques before the hunting season to become proficient and effective.

Grunting techniques can be used to:
- Locate elk

- Bring in bulls

- Bring in cows

- Simulate a dominant bull elk

- Simulate a subordinate bull elk

It's important to note that grunting techniques should be used in combination with other calling techniques, such as bugling, cow calling, and calf calling, to create a more realistic and effective calling sequence.

6. CHIRPING:

Cow elk make a variety of sounds, and chirping is one of them! While it's not as well-known as the bull elk's bugling, cow elk chirping is a real thing.

Cow elk chirping often sounds like a high-pitched, bird-like "tsee" or "tsit" noise. They typically make this sound when:

- Communicating with their calves or other females
- Expressing alarm or alerting others to potential danger
- Signaling friendly interactions, like approaching or greeting each other

This chirping sound is usually softer and more nasal than the bull elk's bugling, and it's a unique way for cow elk to convey information and emotions.

- Mimic the high-pitched chirping sound of a cow or calf elk.

- Use a chirp call or a diaphragm call.

Chirping techniques for calling elk involve simulating the high-pitched, nasal sounds made by cow elk and calves. Here are some chirping techniques:

- The "High-Pitched Chirp":
- Make a high-pitched, nasal "chip" or "chirp" sound.

- Use a soft, gentle tone.

- The "Series Chirp":
- Make a series of high-pitched, nasal chirps.

- Vary pitch and tone.

- The "Chirp and Whine":
- Start with a high-pitched chirp.

- Follow with a soft, nasal whine.

- The "Chirp and Bleat":
- Start with a high-pitched chirp.

- Follow with a soft, nasal bleat.

- The "Calf Chirp":
- Make a high-pitched, nasal "calf-like" sound.

- Use a soft, gentle tone.

- The "Chirp and Pause":

- Make a high-pitched chirp.

- Pause for 10-15 seconds.

- The "Chirp and Move":
- Make a high-pitched chirp.

- Move to a new location and repeat.

- The "Chirp Sequence":
- Make a series of high-pitched chirps.

- Vary tone, pitch, and volume.

Remember to vary your chirping techniques to simulate different cow elk and calves and to keep the elk interested. Also, practice your chirping techniques before the hunting season to become proficient and effective.

Chirping techniques can be used to:
- Locate elk

- Bring in cows

- Bring in bulls

- Simulate a cow elk

- Simulate a calf elk

It's important to note that chirping techniques should be used in combination with other calling techniques, such as bugling, cow calling, and grunting, to create a more realistic and effective calling sequence.

7. CALLING IN DIFFERENT TERRAIN:

Calling elk in different terrain requires adapting your strategies to the environment. Here are some tips:

Open Meadows:
- Use louder, longer calls to carry across open spaces

- Bugle or cow call to locate bulls or attract cows and calves

- Be prepared for elk to respond from a distance

Dense Forest:
- Use softer, more subtle calls to avoid spooking elk

- Focus on cow calls or gentle bugling to mimic close-range communication

- Pay attention to subtle responses, like rustling or snapping

Mountainous Terrain:

- Use calls that echo well, like high-pitched bugling or loud cow calls

- Take advantage of natural amplification, like valleys or canyons

- Be mindful of wind direction and call accordingly

Riparian Areas:

- Use water-friendly calls, like softer bugling or chirping cow calls

- Take advantage of the natural corridor effect, where elk tend to congregate

- Be prepared for elk to move quietly through these areas

Remember:

- Always consider wind direction, time of day, and elk behavior when calling

- Adapt your calling strategy based on the specific terrain and situation

- Practice makes perfect – experiment with different calls and techniques.

STRATEGIES

1. Use calls in combination:
- Use bugling and cow calling together to simulate a bull and cow interaction.

2. Vary your calls:
- Change the tone, pitch, and volume of your calls to sound like different elk.

3. Use calls to locate:
- Make loud calls to locate elk, then switch to softer calls to bring them in.

4. Use calls to stop elk:
- Make a loud call to stop elk in their tracks, giving you a clear shot.

5. Be patient:
- Elk may not respond immediately, so be patient and persistent.

6. Use calls in conjunction with other tactics:
- Use calls with scouting, stalking, and ambush tactics to increase success.

Remember, practice makes perfect, so practice your elk calling techniques before the hunting season to become proficient and effective.

- *Stalking:* Use stealth and camouflage to get close to your target.

- *Ambushing:* Set up in a strategic location and wait for elk to come to you.

- *Driving:* Use a team of hunters to push elk towards a designated area.

- *Hunting Bedding Areas[1]:*
• Make sure you're in tight cover where you won't get spotted. They'll probably come sneaking in.

• Start raking and keep raking.
    • Do some heavy breathing through your bugle tube.

• Give a short bugle.

• Go back to raking and thrashing.

- *Slow Playing a reluctant bull[2]:*
• Do three cow calls, then wait two minutes.

• A few more cow calls and wait again.

• Start raking and thrashing.

• Start heavy panting through your bugle tube and glunking[3].

• Rake aggressively.

• Make a winey cow call.

- He will probably respond with a short round up bugle.

- Respond with heavy mouth grunt.

- Call him over with escalated cow calls, longer and louder.

- Keep raking this whole time.

- Cut off any response with an aggressive bugle.

If a bull answers a cow call, he is trying to call her over.
 [1,2] *taken from ElkNut Outdoors elk calling conference on YouTube.*

[3] *Elk glunking is a sound made by bull elk to locate cow elk. It is a deep-toned, muffled-sounding guttural call bulls make when they are nearby cows. It sounds something like a bass drum sitting in water, and although not as common as bugles and chuckles, this sound can travel far due to the low frequency.*

Glunking:

- Glunking is a sure sign that a bull either has cows or believes that cows are in the immediate vicinity that he might be able to control.

- Many folks that are familiar with the vocalization recognize that glunks are associated with cows, but many mistakenly associate glunks with all sorts of things: ranging from a bull trying to attract cows or pull cows away from another bull, all the way to a vocalization used by a bull trying to intimidate another bull.

- Their real meaning, however, is pretty straightforward, and actually quite simple, if you understand a little about bull behavior. He is trying to entice any cows in the area to come over to him.

To replicate the glunking sound, slap the palm of your hand against the mouth end of your bugle tube, pointing the tube in the direction you want the sound to travel.

5

Elk Hunting Tips

Additional tips to increase your chances of success:

- Pay attention to wind direction and scent control.

Wind direction and scent control are crucial factors to consider when hunting elk. Elk have an incredibly keen sense of smell, which they use to detect potential threats, find food, and communicate with each other.

Elk have a highly developed olfactory system, with a large nasal cavity and a high concentration of olfactory receptors. This allows them to detect scents that are too faint for humans to detect. In fact, an elk's sense of smell is estimated to be 1,000 times more sensitive than a human's.

Elk nasal conchae: The turbinate bones are shaped like scrolls or conchae, which increase the surface area for air to pass over, allowing for more efficient warming and humidification.

When hunting elk, it's essential to consider the wind direction and take steps to control your scent. Here are some tips:

Dead Down Wind - Wind Checker
Cabelas.ca

1. Pay attention to wind **direction:** Always check the wind direction before heading out on a hunt. Try to position yourself so that the wind is in your face, carrying your scent away from the elk. I always carry wind checker powder. This is a scentless white powder to detect wind direction.

2. Use scent-control products: There are many scent-control products available, such as sprays, powders, and clothing, that can help minimize your scent. Another thing I use frequently is scent sticks. These small sticks, when lit, emit the odor of cow elk. Another thing they do is provide a constant wind direction indication.

3. Wear clean clothes: Make sure your clothes are clean and free of any strong scents. Avoid wearing clothes that have been washed in fragrant detergents or dryer sheets.

4. Avoid strong-smelling foods: Avoid eating strong-smelling foods, such as garlic or onions, before heading out on a hunt.

5. Keep your gear clean: Make sure your gear, including your rifle and backpack, are clean and free of any strong scents.

6. Use a scent-free tree stand: If you're using a tree stand, make sure it's scent-free. Avoid using tree stands that have been treated with chemicals or have a strong scent.

7. Be mindful of your body odor: Make sure you're physically clean and free of any strong body odor.

By paying attention to wind direction and taking steps to control your scent, you can increase your chances of getting close to elk and making a successful hunt. Although it is impossible to completely cover your scent, anything you can do to give you an advantage can pay off in the end.

Tinks –Smokin' Sticks
Cabelas.ca

Remember, elk have a keen sense of smell, and even the slightest scent can alert them to your presence. There is a saying in the elk hunting world, "An elk will hear you three times, see you twice, but smell you only once." Once you are winded, they will not need to see you, they will bolt. Smell is their most trusted of the five senses.

- Use optics to spot and track elk from a distance.

Using optics, such as binoculars or spotting scopes, to spot and track elk from a distance offers several advantages:

1. Increased visibility: Optics allow you to see elk from a much greater distance than the naked eye, making it easier to locate and track them. A good investment is a spotting scope or a pair of binoculars. For safety reasons, never use your rifle scope for spotting.

Hunter using binoculars

2. Early detection: With optics, you can detect elk movement and activity from a distance, giving you a head start on tracking and stalking.

3. Reduced disturbance: By observing elk from a distance, you can avoid spooking them, allowing you to get closer without alerting them to your presence.

4. Better understanding of elk behavior: Observing elk from a distance with optics allows you to study their behavior, movement patterns, and habitat use, making you a more effective hunter.

5. Timesaving: Optics can help you quickly scan large areas, saving time and energy in your search for elk.

6. Accurate identification: Optics enable you to identify elk more accurately, helping you distinguish between bulls and cows, and identify specific characteristics like antler size and shape.

7. Enhanced safety: By observing from a distance, you can assess potential dangers like bull elk behavior or terrain difficulties before approaching.

8. *Improved stalking:* With optics, you can plan a more effective stalking route, taking into account elk movement and terrain features.

9. *Increased success:* Using optics to spot and track elk from a distance can significantly increase your chances of a successful hunt.

10. *Enjoyment:* Observing elk from a distance with optics can be a thrilling and rewarding experience, allowing you to appreciate these magnificent animals in their natural habitat. By utilizing optics to spot and track elk from a distance, you can gain a significant advantage in your hunting endeavors, while also enhancing your overall hunting experience.

- Be patient and persistent – elk hunting can be challenging.

Being patient and persistent is crucial when elk hunting, as it can be a challenging and unpredictable pursuit. Here are some reasons why patience and persistence are essential:

1. *Elk are elusive:* Elk are skilled at hiding and can be difficult to locate, even for experienced hunters.

2. *Long days:* Elk hunting often involves long days of glassing, hiking, and waiting, requiring mental and physical endurance.

3. *Unpredictable weather:* Weather conditions can change quickly, affecting elk behavior and making hunting conditions challenging.

A hunter taking a break after a long day

4. Changing elk behavior: Elk behavior can change rapidly due to various factors like hunting pressure, weather, and food availability.

5. Missed opportunities: Even experienced hunters can miss shots or encounter elk that are not receptive to hunting. Read one of my experiences at the end of this book.

6. Physical demands: Elk hunting requires physical stamina, as hunters may need to hike long distances and navigate challenging terrain.

7. Mental toughness: Elk hunting can be mentally demanding, requiring focus, discipline, and emotional control.

8. Adaptability: Hunters need to be adaptable and adjust their strategies based on changing conditions and elk behavior.

9. Learning from failures: Persistence allows hunters to learn from missed opportunities and apply those lessons to future hunts.

10. Rewarding experience: The thrill of harvesting an elk after days or even weeks of effort makes the experience incredibly rewarding.

To cultivate patience and persistence when elk hunting:

- Set realistic expectations

- Focus on the process, not just the outcome

- Stay positive and motivated

- Take breaks and rest when needed

- Stay hydrated and energized

- Continuously learn and improve skills

- Embrace the challenge and enjoy the journey

By embracing patience and persistence, elk hunters can increase their chances of success and create a more fulfilling and memorable hunting experience.

BE ETHICAL

- Respect the animal and the environment – follow ethical hunting practices.

Respect for the animal and the environment is crucial while hunting, as it ensures a safe, ethical, and sustainable hunting experience. Ethical hunting practices are essential to maintain the balance between hunting and conservation. Here are some key aspects:

Respect for the Animal:

1. Harvest what you need: Only take what you can use, avoiding wastage and excess killing.

2. Quick and humane kill: Ensure a swift and painless death, minimizing suffering. This required good marksmanship, so being familiar with your equipment and practicing is crucial.

3. Handle with care: Treat the animal with respect, avoiding unnecessary damage or mistreatment.

4. Use as much as possible: Utilize as much of the animal as possible, reducing waste and honoring its sacrifice. Most areas will have laws in place for what parts of the animal you are required to take.

Field dressing an elk
Helen Klassen

5. Be familiar with field dressing an animal: There are different methods to do this. I prefer what is called 'the gutless method.' It is the cleanest and doesn't require to hang the animal. Some people avoid this method because they think you can't get the tenderloins out this way. There is a simple trick I use (see my YouTube channel PK Alberta Hunting).

Respect for the Environment:

1. Follow regulations: Adhere to laws and guidelines protecting habitats, wildlife, and ecosystems.

2. Minimize impact: Avoid damaging the environment, including vegetation, water sources, and soil.

3. Leave no trace: Remove all trash, and leave the area as found. One of my pet peeves is finding trash in the bush left by other hunters. Unless your mother is hunting with you and picking up after you, pick up your trash and carry it out.

4. Support conservation: Contribute to organizations and initiatives preserving wildlife habitats and populations.

Ethical Hunting Practices:

1. Fair chase: Hunt animals in their natural habitat, without unfair advantage or manipulation.

2. Identification: Ensure accurate identification of the species, age, and sex before harvesting.

3. Shot placement: Aim for a quick and humane kill, avoiding unnecessary suffering.

4. Hunting licenses: Obtain required permits and follow bag limits to maintain sustainable populations.

5. Hunting ethics courses: Take courses to learn and refresh knowledge on ethical hunting practices.

6. Mentorship: Guide new hunters, sharing knowledge and promoting ethical practices.

7. Respect for other users: Share public lands with other users, such as hikers and wildlife viewers.

8. Reporting: Report illegal or unethical hunting activities to authorities.

By embracing respect for the animal and the environment, hunters can ensure a sustainable and ethical hunting experience, preserving wildlife populations and ecosystems for future generations.

More Bugles
Helen Klassen

6

Elk Biology and Habitat

Understanding elk biology and habitat is crucial for successful hunting. Here are some key facts:

- Elk are ruminants, feeding on grasses, shrubs, and trees.

Here are some interesting facts about elk as ruminants:

- ***Ruminantia:*** Ruminants belong to the suborder Ruminantia, which are able to acquire nutrients from plant-based food by fermenting it in a specialized stomach prior to digestion, principally through microbial actions.

- ***Foregut fermentation:*** The process, which takes place in the front part of the digestive system and therefore is called foregut fermentation, typically requires the fermented ingesta (known as cud) to be regurgitated and chewed again.

Relaxing and chewing cud

- **Rumination:** The process of rechewing the cud to further break down plant matter and stimulate digestion is called rumination.

- **Fermentation:** Ruminants have four stomachs in order to help with the digestion of the grass and leaves which form the majority of their diet.

- **Cud:** Ruminants regurgitate food from the first stomach back into their mouths as "cud". It is then chewed thoroughly before being passed along to the other stomachs.

- **Diet:** Elk are herbivorous, and their diet consists of grass and leaves. In addition to grass and leaves, the elk eats tree bark, particularly in winter when food is scarce. In spring it forages on sprouting saplings. An elk eats an average of around 20 lb. (9.1 kg) of plant matter every day.

- *They have an incredible sense of smell.*

Elk possess an incredibly keen sense of smell, which plays a vital role in their survival and daily life. Here are some fascinating facts about elk and their sense of smell:

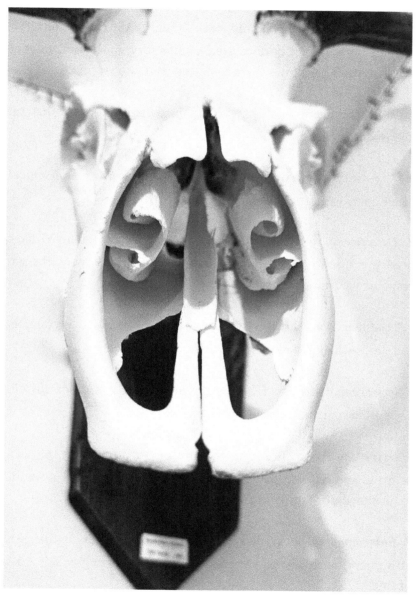

Elk nasal conchae –rolled up like a scroll
Helen Klassen

1. Acute olfactory system: Elk have a highly developed olfactory system, with a large surface area of olfactory epithelium in their nasal cavity. This allows them to detect even faint scents.

2. Sensitive nostrils: Elk have highly sensitive nostrils that can detect subtle changes in scent particles in the air.

3. Long-distance detection: Elk can detect scents from great distances, often up to 1 mile (1.6 km) away.

4. Detection of predators: Elk use their sense of smell to detect predators like wolves, bears, and mountain lions, allowing them to respond accordingly.

5. Food detection: Elk rely on their sense of smell to locate food sources, such as grasses, shrubs, and trees.

6. Social communication: Elk use scent marking to communicate with each other, particularly during the mating season.

7. Urine and feces: Elk use their sense of smell to detect the scent of urine and feces from other elk, helping them identify potential mates, rivals, or family members.

8. Environmental awareness: Elk can detect changes in their environment, such as the presence of humans, through their sense of smell.

9. Adaptation to wind: Elk have adapted to wind conditions, using their sense of smell to detect scents carried by the wind.

*10. **Superior to humans:*** Elk's sense of smell is estimated to be 100-1,000 times more sensitive than that of humans.

Remember, elk's incredible sense of smell is a vital tool for their survival and social behavior, making them one of the most impressive animals in the wild.

- They require large habitats with adequate food, water, and shelter.

- Elk are sensitive to human disturbance and habitat fragmentation

The average size of an elk herd habitat can vary greatly depending on factors such as location, terrain, and availability of food and water. However, here are some general guidelines:
    - In the western United States, elk habitats can range from 100 to 500 square miles (260 to 1,300 square kilometers).

- In areas with abundant food and water, elk habitats might be smaller, around 50 to 200 square miles (130 to 520 square kilometers).

- In areas with limited resources or harsh terrain, elk habitats can be much larger, up to 1,000 square miles (2,600 square kilometers) or more.

It's important to note that elk are highly mobile and can travel long distances in search of food, water, and suitable habitat, so their actual habitat size can vary greatly over the course of a year.

7

Conservation and
Management

Elk hunting is not just about harvesting an animal; it's also about conservation and management. Here are some key points:

- Elk populations are managed by wildlife agencies to ensure sustainability. Wildlife agencies manage elk populations sustainably through the following methods:

- ***Monitoring data:*** Wildlife agencies collect harvest data from hunters, which helps them understand trends in elk populations and make informed decisions about conservation efforts.

- ***Harvest management:*** Elk harvests are managed through a system of licenses, quotas, and restrictions to ensure that hunting does not harm elk populations. The system of licenses, quotas, and restrictions for elk hunting in Canada includes:

- *Licenses:* Hunters must have an Outdoors Card, an elk license, and an elk tag for the appropriate season, harvest area, and type of elk. Non-residents are not allowed to hunt elk in some provinces.

- *Quotas:* In some areas, elk tags are limited, and hunters must apply through a draw system. Successful applicants are assigned a tag, and quotas vary by area and type of elk (bull or cow).

- *Restrictions:* Hunters must follow rules for tagging and transporting harvested elk, and there are specific regulations for firearms, party hunting, and hunting on private property.

Alberta hunting tag

- *Hunting Seasons:* Elk hunting seasons vary by province and Wildlife Management Unit (WMU), with specific dates for residents and non-residents.

- *Bag Limits:* Hunters are limited to one elk per tag, and there may be restrictions on the type of elk that can be harvested (e.g., size, bull, or cow).

- **Hunting Methods:** There are restrictions on hunting methods, such as the use of bait or dogs, and hunters must follow guidelines for fair chase and ethical hunting practices.

- **Age and Sex:** Hunters may be required to harvest elk of a specific age or sex, and there may be restrictions on the harvesting of calves or dependent young.

- **Private Property:** Hunters must obtain written consent from land-owners before hunting on private property. This has saved me one time. I had a written consent letter for a certain field I was hunting, and a Wildlife officer came along and checked it out. Because of the letter, there were no further questions. Funny story, I found out later that the person who had given me the letter was not the actual landowner. He just wanted me away from public land that he was hunting. Lesson learned, do your own due diligence.

- **Reporting:** Hunters may be required to report their harvest, including the location, date, and type of elk harvested. It is important to file a harvest report, even if not required by law. This is helpful information for wildlife agencies about population, habitat, and behavior.

- **Aerial surveys:** Wildlife agencies conduct aerial surveys to monitor elk populations and track changes over time. Aerial surveys are a common method used by wildlife agencies to monitor elk populations. Here are some points that expand on this:

- **Infrequent surveys:** Aerial surveys are conducted infrequently, typically only once every 10 years, due to the high cost of aerial monitoring.

- *Population monitoring:* Aerial surveys are used to monitor elk populations, including population size, distribution, and trends.

- *Habitat assessment:* Aerial surveys can also be used to assess elk habitat, including the quality and quantity of habitat, and the impact of human activities on elk habitat.

- *Data analysis:* Data collected from aerial surveys is analyzed to inform elk management decisions, including setting harvest quotas, and developing conservation plans.

- *Combination* with other methods: Aerial surveys are often combined with other methods, such as ground surveys and hunter surveys, to provide a more comprehensive understanding of elk populations.

- *Challenges:* Aerial surveys can be challenging, particularly in areas with dense vegetation or rugged terrain, and may require specialized equipment and expertise.

- *Cost-effective:* Aerial surveys can be a cost-effective method for monitoring elk populations over large areas, particularly when compared to ground surveys.

- *Real-time data:* Aerial surveys can provide real-time data, which can be useful for making timely management decisions.

- *Collaboration:* Aerial surveys can be conducted in collaboration with other agencies, organizations, and stakeholders, which can help to share resources and expertise.

- Predator management: Wildlife agencies manage predator populations, such as wolves, grizzly bears, and cougars, to ensure they do not harm elk populations.

A cougar that was accidently caught in a wolf snare
Helen Klassen

Predator management by wildlife agencies to protect elk populations involves regulating the numbers and impact of predators such as:

1. Wolves:

2. Bears:

3. Cougars:

4. Coyotes:

Predator populations are managed through hunting, trapping, and control measures to reduce elk calf predation.

5. Other predators: Other predators like bobcats, lynx, and wolverines are also managed to reduce their impact on elk populations.
Management strategies include:

1. Monitoring predator populations and elk-predator interactions.

2. Setting predator harvest quotas and seasons.

3. Relocating problem predators.

4. Conducting control measures like lethal removal or non-lethal

A wildlife officer studies a map

deterrents.

5. Collaborating with landowners, hunters, and other stakeholders.

6. Researching effective management techniques.

7. Educating the public about predator management and elk conservation.

These efforts aim to strike a balance between predator and prey populations, maintaining a healthy and sustainable elk population while also considering the ecological role of predators.

HABITAT MANAGEMENT

Wildlife agencies work to maintain and restore elk habitats, such as forests and grasslands, to support healthy elk populations. Wildlife agencies play a crucial role in maintaining and restoring elk habitats through:

1. Habitat conservation: Protecting and acquiring critical elk habitats, such as migration corridors, winter ranges, and calving grounds.

2. Habitat restoration: Restoring degraded or damaged habitats, like wetlands, meadows, and forests, to improve elk forage and shelter.

3. Land management: Collaborating with private landowners and other agencies to implement conservation practices, like prescribed burning, thinning, and re-vegetation.

4. Wildlife-friendly infrastructure: Modifying or removing infrastructure, like fences and culverts, to improve elk movement and access to habitats.

5. Invasive species management: Controlling non-native species, like cheatgrass and knapweed, that compete with native vegetation and degrade elk habitats.

6. Prescribed fire: Conducting controlled burns to maintain healthy forests, reduce fuel loads, and promote regrowth of elk forage.

7. Elk-friendly forestry: Promoting sustainable forestry practices that maintain elk habitat quality and connectivity.

8. Wetland management: Protecting and restoring wetlands, like elk watering holes and riparian areas, crucial for elk survival.

9. Monitoring and research: Studying elk habitat use, monitoring habitat conditions, and researching effective conservation strategies.

10. Partnerships and collaborations: Working with other agencies, organizations, and stakeholders to leverage resources, expertise, and funding for elk habitat conservation and restoration.

By taking these steps, wildlife agencies help ensure the long-term health and sustainability of elk populations and their habitats.

- Research and collaboration: Wildlife agencies collaborate with researchers and other organizations to better understand elk ecology and develop effective conservation strategies.

- Regulations and enforcement: Wildlife agencies establish and enforce regulations to prevent overhunting and ensure that elk populations remain sustainable.

- Public engagement and education: Wildlife agencies engage with

the public to raise awareness about elk conservation and promote sustainable hunting practices.

- Hunters play a crucial role in elk conservation through license fees and harvest data.

- Support conservation efforts and respect wildlife regulations.

8

Conclusion

By following the tips and strategies outlined in this book, you'll be well on your way to a successful elk hunting adventure.

In conclusion, I hope that the knowledge and experiences shared within these pages has inspired and empowered you to embark on your own elk hunting adventures. Elk hunting is a challenging and rewarding pursuit that requires patience, persistence, and a deep respect for these magnificent creatures and their habitats.

Throughout this book, I have covered a range of topics, from preparation and planning to tactics and strategies for success.

I have explored the importance of understanding elk behavior, habitat, and migration patterns, as well as the need for physical conditioning and mental toughness. I have also delved into the world of elk calling, stalking, and shooting, providing tips and techniques to help you close the deal.

But elk hunting is more than just a physical and technical challenge – it is also a spiritual and emotional journey. It is an opportunity to connect with nature, to test ourselves, and to experience the thrill of the hunt. It is a chance to learn, to grow, and to develop a deeper appreciation for the natural world and our place within it.

Bull elk grazing
Helen Klassen

As you set out on your own elk hunting adventures, remember to always prioritize safety, ethics, and respect for the animals and the land.

Remember to be patient, persistent, and humble, and to never stop learning and improving. And most importantly, remember to enjoy the journey, to soak up the experiences, and to cherish the memories that elk hunting provides.

In the end, elk hunting is not just about harvesting an animal –it

is about the journey, the experience, and the connections we make along the way. It is about the camaraderie with fellow hunters, the guidance from mentors, and the lessons learned from the elk themselves. It is about the thrill of the hunt, the rush of adrenaline, and the sense of accomplishment that comes with success. For myself, I always come away with a
new appreciation and adoration for our Creator God and His wonderous world He allows us to enjoy.

I hope that this book has inspired you to embark on your own elk hunting journey, and that the tips and techniques shared within its pages will help you to succeed. But most importantly, I hope that you will always remember to respect the animals, the land, and the experience – and to never stop enjoying the journey. Happy hunting!

Remember to always prioritize safety, ethics, and conservation.

9

Epilogue

The sun was slowly rising over the treetops, casting a golden glow over the forest. I had been waiting for this moment for weeks, and finally it was here. This was my sixth year chasing elk, with each previous year having ended in disappointment. But here it was, a new season, a new opportunity. I was slowing making my way along a well used game trail just off a private farm field that I knew was frequented by elk, rifle at the ready, scanning the field for any sign of elk.

Suddenly, a loud bugle stopped me in my tracks. I gave a short cow call in response, and I heard him coming in. He was out in front of me to the right, maybe about 80 yards away.

Today might be the day," I thought. All these years of frusration and disappointment might finally pay off.

Then, just off to my left where another trail joined up with this one, I heard movement. I crouched down, gave another cow call and I could see movement through the trees. To my surprise, out stepped a young bull. The first bull, now to my right, was still bugling occasionally, but my focus now was on the one right in front of me. He stopped not more than 10 yards away, staring right at me. He wasn't big, a young 4x4 but I wasn't after a trophy. I had been chasing these majestic animals for six years and size did not matter.

I didn't want to take a frontal shot with a rifle, so I waited, looking at him through my scope. There was a stare off for about 15 – 20 seconds, and then he slowly turned to walk away. He wasn't spooked, just sensed that something wasn't right. As he turned broadside, my heart was racing as I took aim from just 10 yards away. I squeezed the trigger, but instead of the expected crack of the rifle, I heard a sickening silence. I had forgotten to release the trigger lock!

I frantically tried to pull the lock back, but it was too late. The elk, by this time was fully turned around and walking away. I was left sitting in stunned silence, my heart heavy with disappointment.

I couldn't believe it. I had been so close, and now the opportunity was gone. I took a deep breath, trying to shake off the frustration. I knew I had to stay focused, there could be another chance.

I waited a few moments after he was out of sight, and because he hadn't appeared spooked, I decided to follow him.

The crisp autumn air filled my lungs as I crept through the forest, my rifle at the ready again. I followed for about 50 yards or so and stopped for some soft cow calls. The first bull, now behind me, sounded off again. He sounded bigger and for a moment I hesitated and contemplated pursuing him instead.

Before I had much time to think about it, there was another small bull just off to my left again. I could hear the one I was following still walk in front of me, and now another one peering at me through the underbrush. He was making his way past me, trying to get down wind.

Now I had three bulls, all within a short distance. It was the most intense elk experience I had ever had, and it was all coming together, it was really going to happen, I could feel it.

The third bull eventually got past and winded me. I was watching it slowly moving past, it's head down low, peering at me through the underbrush. There was no shot available, and inevitably it caught my scent and just disappeared.

'Now, focus back on the one you followed," I told myself. He was still moving about, just out of sight. I positioned myself against a tree and waited, doing a few soft cow calls. There was a small clearing, about 30 yards across and I was hoping he would step out.

I was back and forth with this young bull for what seemed like at least an hour, but it was probably more like 15 minutes. He finally did come out into the clearing, but of course he stopped right where a hung-up dead fall was right across his vitals.

"Just one more step," I urged him in my head. Again, I had my scope on him and was just waiting. Finally, he took one more step and I had him in my sights. He was 30 yards away broadside.

I took a deep breath, steadied my aim, and squeezed the trigger. A metallic 'CLICK' was all I heard. What? I couldn't believe it! My second chance on this same bull, and again I was foiled. It was a dud bullet. By the time I chambered another round, the elk was gone. When I picked up the bullet from the ground, I could see the firing pin had fired, but the primer hadn't gone off.

My dud bullet
Helen Klassen

The disappointment almost matched the time a few weeks earlier when I had wounded an elk and had been unable to recover him. I was devastated. I was starting to think that an elk for me just wasn't going to happen. It was a sobering reminder that even with the best equipment and skills, things don't always go as planned. This elk lived to roam another day, never knowing how close it had come to being my prey that day, TWICE.

So, with all the disappointments, missed opportunities, should-haves and could-haves that come with elk hunting, we never give up. Stay positive, keep your head up, rest up and regroup, and see you in the elk woods.

PS. I did get my first elk a short time later that season

Bull elk in velvet
Helen Klassen

Printed in the USA
CPSIA information can be obtained
at www.ICGtesting.com
LVHW020825030924
789973LV00003B/23